You're
Amazing!

By Mark Pichora

[Starring you]

For Léo

 FriesenPress

Suite 300 - 990 Fort St
Victoria, BC, V8V 3K2
Canada

www.friesenpress.com

ISBN
978-1-4602-9105-4 (Hardcover)
978-1-4602-8047-8 (Paperback)
978-1-4602-8048-5 (eBook)

1. Juvenile Nonfiction, Science & Nature, Anatomy & Physiology

Distributed to the trade by The Ingram Book Company

Excuse me, dear friend,
could I borrow your ear?

I have a great story
I think you should hear!

This story is *special.*
This story is *true.*
This story is *big!*

And it's all about you!

And although it's wrapped up in some
big fancy phrasing,

Its message, quite simply, is
you are amazing!

Amazingly great!
And in case you'd not heard,

My friends have come with me
to help spread the word!

Meet Joanie and Leo.
They're Lumins, like you.

And my name is Louie!
And **I'm Lumin too!**

Amazing you are,
from your head to your toe!

And if you don't believe me,
well prove that it's so!

You have eyes that can See
and a nose that can Smell,

And two ears that can Hear.
And they hear very well!

You have skin that can Feel the warm breeze from the south,
And a tongue that can Taste and make words with your mouth.

Your incredible body has so many quirks!
Haven't you wondered just how it all works?

3

Let's begin with your feet.
They are really quite neat!

If you wash them with soap,
they will smell like a treat!

On the surface, you'd think
they were simple and plain,

Just for stepping and stomping
and splashing the rain.

But inside they have such an **astounding design!**

They have twenty-six bones, each one sculpted so fine!

So take care of your feet and do not stub your toes.

They won't like it one bit, as 'most everyone knows!

Your Legs are up next,
and they're perfectly built

For jumping and dancing
and running full-tilt!

You have four bones each leg,
and the Big one up high

Is a bone called the *femur*,
which sits in your thigh.

Your legs are so Strong,
they'll lift double your weight!

Your legs are so Quick
that you'll never be late!

They can carry you fast.
They can carry you slow!

And they'll take you wherever
you tell them to go!

You can hike over mountains that reach for the sky,
Or through deep, rocky canyons and deserts so dry.

You just put on your boots and then tie up your laces,
And let your legs take you to all of these places!

But for all of the wonderful things they can do,
They are just a small part of incredible you!

You also have two of my favorite things.
In fact, I dare say that they're better than wings!

But let's make this more fun. Let me give you a clue!
A riddle like this should be easy for you!

You can count on these things.
They are nimble, yet strong.

Only one of them's right,
and yet neither is wrong!

You have only one left,
but you always have two.

Can you guess what they are?
They're your Hands, buckaroo!

There are **Lots** of great things
you can do with your hands!

You can play the guitar and
make **Millions** of fans!

You can build a new house.
Way up high, in a tree!

You can swing from a rope,
and then dive in the sea!

But they'll do even more!
They'll do thrilling new feats!

They'll scrub all the toilets
and fold all the sheets!

12

You are full of great wonder
and all would agree,

But most wondrous of all are
the things we can't see!

Like, what keeps you going?
And what keeps you growing?

What happens inside?
There's some stuff that's worth knowing!

Your body needs food! And your STOMACH knows best.
He'll rumble and grumble and boldly request...

"Give me **Food**, please! **A meal!** You really must **Eat!**
I've a job to get done and a quota to meet!

I break down your food, mush it up, get it packed,
And I send it on down through your **digestive tract!**

Your body has needs and although it seems foul,
Your bloodstream gets nutrients straight from your bowel!

Sometimes it's messy, and toxins get through,
But I try to get most of that out with your poo.

That is my job and I'm sure to deliver!
If ya wanna know more, you can speak to your **Liver!**"

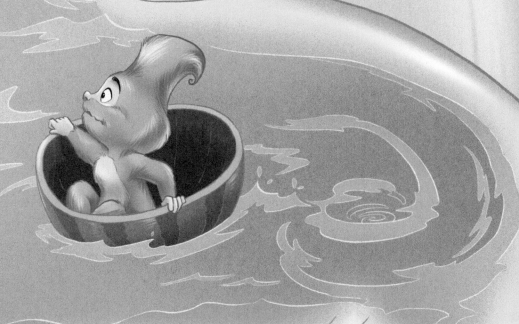

"Oh, Hi! I'm your Liver!
I'm so, so delighted!

...To Meet you!
...Like science? ...I get so excited!

I try to be humble, but lately I've found
That my skills as a chemist are rather renowned!

I have *several* jobs and I work day and night!
And I do them so you can keep feeling just right!

I get blood from my friends, and they're quite a fine crew,
Your intestines, your spleen, and your pancreas, too!

They send me their blood, and it's loaded with stuff,
From the food that you eat
...And i can't get enough!

Carbohydrates and Proteins and Sugars and Fat,
I collect and refine and I process all that!

These compounds are fuel for your body to burn,
And you need them around or your engine won't turn!

So I make them and shape them and keep them in store,
And I measure them out when your bloodstream needs more.

But that isn't all, sir! No, I am not through!
I do even more, my dear friend, just for you!

I am also your station for Purification,
Toxin filtration and waste mitigation!

The bad I expel and the good I extract.
Rest assured that my science is always exact!

It's a mighty big job, though, to filter your blood.
If I didn't have help, you'd be in for it, bud!

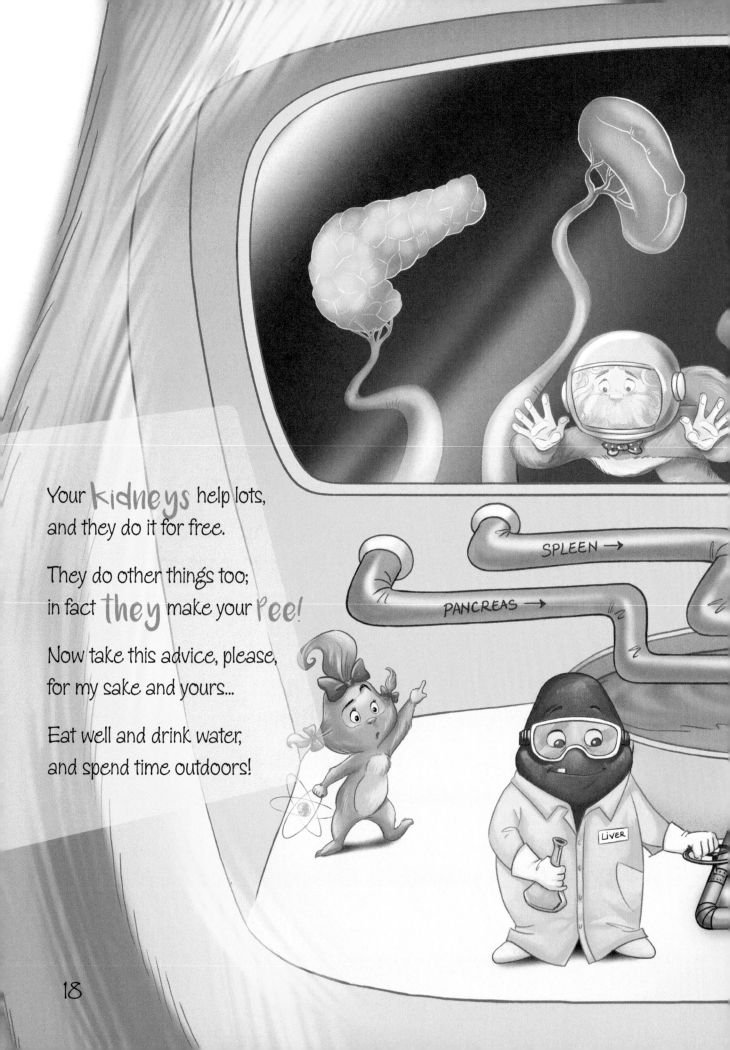

Your kidneys help lots,
and they do it for free.

They do other things too;
in fact they make your pee!

Now take this advice, please,
for my sake and yours...

Eat well and drink water,
and spend time outdoors!

SPLEEN →

PANCREAS →

LIVER

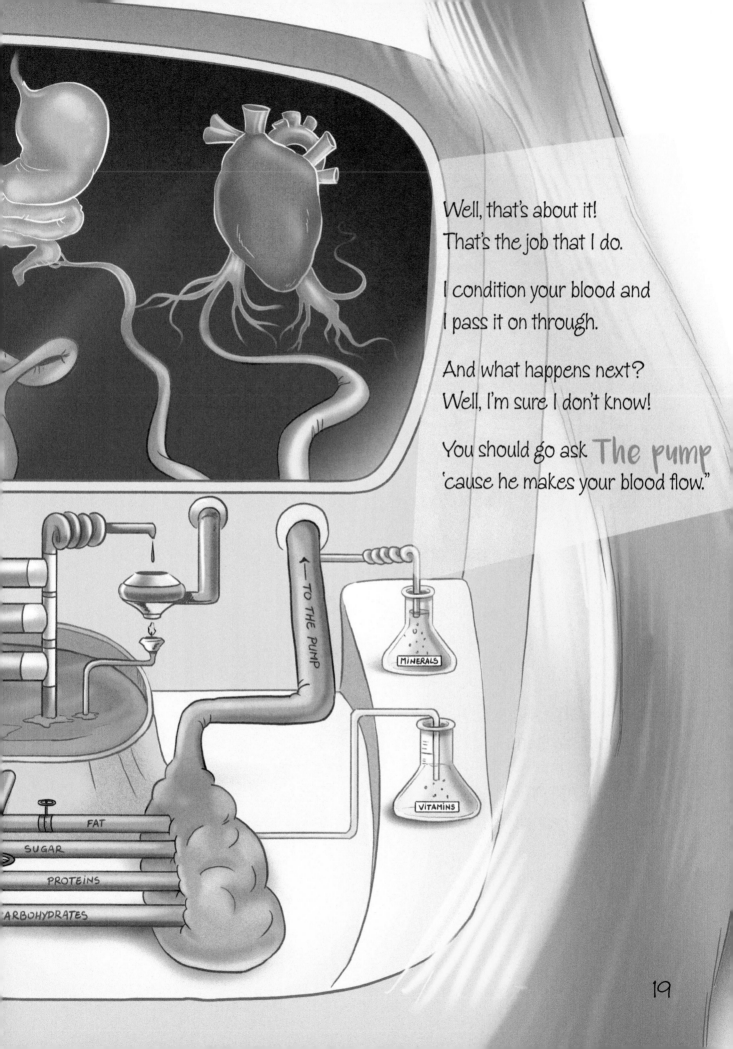

Well, that's about it!
That's the job that I do.

I condition your blood and
I pass it on through.

And what happens next?
Well, I'm sure I don't know!

You should go ask The pump
'cause he makes your blood flow."

"What did he call me!
The pump'? No respect!
'Heart' is my name
and it's 'Heart' I expect!

My goodness, that Liver! He never gets out.
If he did, he would *know* just what I'm all about!

I'm Famous! A big shot!
I don't say it meekly!

That's me on the cover of
Your Organs Weekly!

So what is it like, you ask,
being your heart?

I'm so glad you asked!
Let's begin from the start...

I'm the size of your fist,
and I'm lean and I'm fit!

And I beat day and night,
and I don't ever quit!

No time-outs, no sick days,
no snow days, no rest!

If you're looking for me,
I'll be here in your chest!

I don't stop to take breaks.
I don't stop to smell flowers.

I don't use the loo,
and I do not take showers!

I beat about seventy times in a minute,
And I hope you like math 'cause I'm 'bout to get in it...

That's one hundred Thousand
heartbeats in a day,

And thirty-six Million
from June until May!

Now, I know you're quite smart,
and your brain is a quicky,

But please listen close
'cause this next part is tricky!

Inside I'm divided in
four separate spaces.

Four **muscular** chambers
through which your blood races.

They squeeze and contract,
and they **push** the blood through,

Like a river of nutrients
flowing through you.

First I get blood from your lungs.
And it's Lush!
It's Oxygen-rich, but it's not in a rush...

So I give it a squeeze and I pump it all out.
And it flows through your body,
all 'round and throughout!

It arrives at each muscle,
each fiber, each bone,
It arrives at each tissue that you've ever grown!

It shows up to your outermost, farthest-flung bits,
As well as your innermost smelly armpits!

And when it arrives, it delivers a gift.
It powers your muscles, and gives them a lift!

And then it comes back to me, closing the loop,
But at this point its pressure is starting to droop!

And worse, it's all blue! In a sad sort of state,
And it's looking quite grim as it flows through my gate!

It says, Heart! I need oxygen! Quick! It's all gone!
Send me to Lung; this can not wait 'til dawn!'

So I bow and I flex and I give it a wink,
And I say, 'but of course,
you'll be there in a blink!'

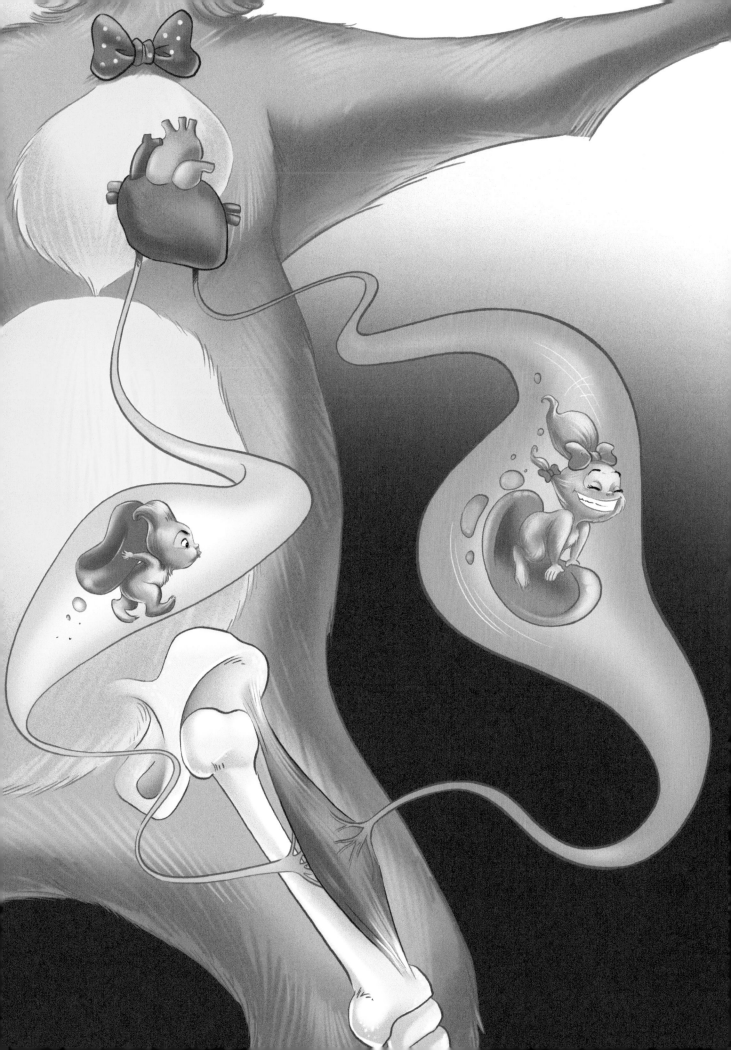

Then I squeeze and contract with bravado and flair,
And I usher your blood to your lungs for more air.

And when it comes back to me, Lo and behold,
It's charged up with oxygen, better than gold!

Now, you've probably noticed, since you are so smart,
That we've gone in a loop now! We're back at the start!

And that's how I work! See? The cycle repeats!
I keep your blood flowing with each of my beats!

Now, there's no need to thank me. I do this for fun!
But of course, if you *really* must thank me, then Run!

Because I like to Move and to Sweat and to Play!
So take me outside because that makes my day!

Now there's one other organ I think you should meet.
Say hello to your Lungs! They are spongy and sweet!"

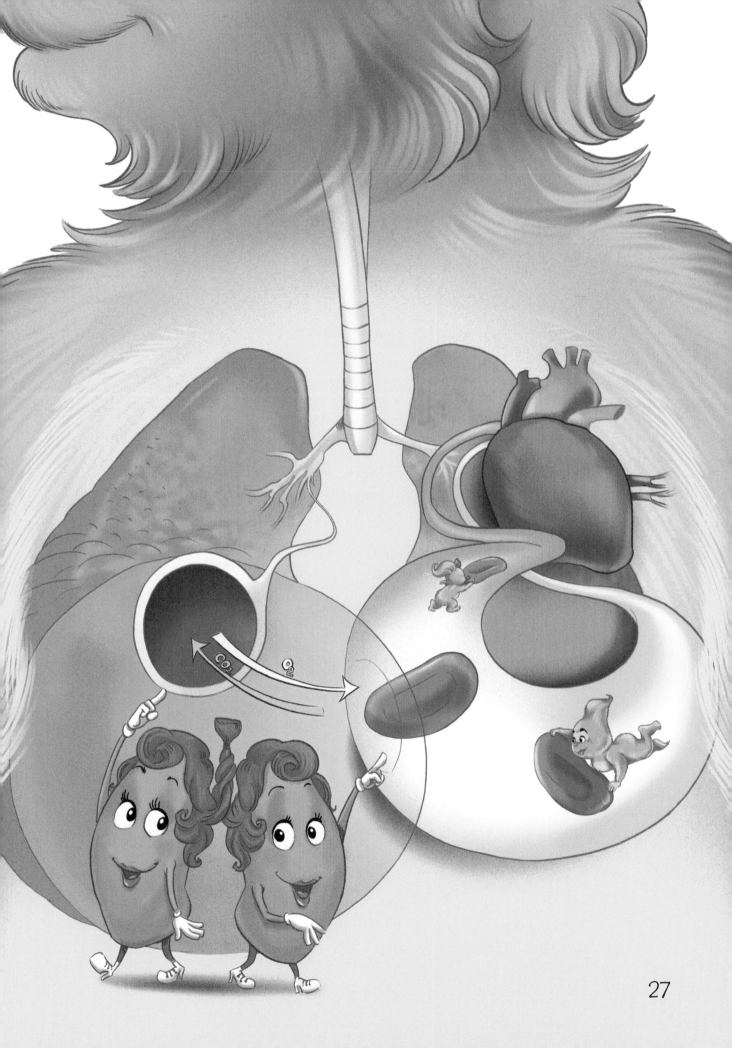

"Yes, hello, we're your Lungs! Oh my gosh! Is it you?
Can we tell you a little about what we do?

Our purpose is simple. It's basic as mud.
We're here to put oxygen into your blood!

We breathe in some air and we slosh it about,
We absorb all the oxygen then we breathe out.

And we work very simply. No knick-knacks or sprockets!
Just six hundred million wee little air pockets!

But we'd just ask a favour, and this is no joke,
Please, please, please, Please promise Don't ever smoke!

And that's about all that we wanted to say,
So remember to breathe, and please have a nice day!"

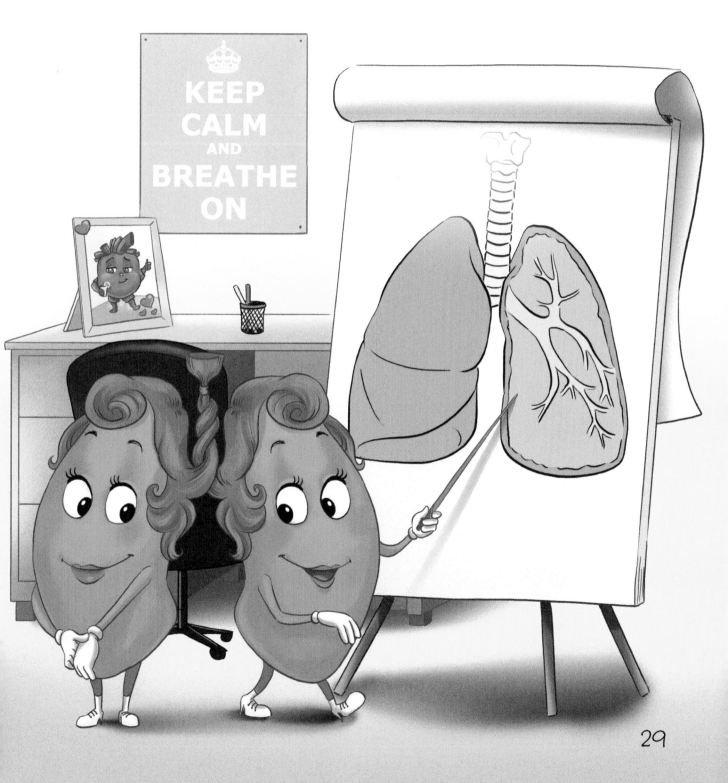

Amazing you are, on the inside and out!
And I hope that by now, we've erased any doubt!

I hope the next time that you see your reflection,
The thing you see first is the Purest perfection!

Now, I'll try to slow down
'cause I know I've said lots,

And you must have some questions!
Some comments! Some thoughts!

You might wonder
"Well shucks, don't you think I'm too frail?
I'm really quite tiny, compared to a whale!"

Whales are enormous! They're kings of the sea!
But you can do more! You can climb up a tree!

"Well, what about bears? And the birds in the sky?
With their rumbling and roaring and soaring so high?

And don't forget monkeys! Yeah, sure, I can climb,
But they'll get up my tree and in just half the time!"

Monkeys are really great climbers, it's true.
Does that come as a shock? They're related to you!

They're also quite smart but don't trouble your mind,
As Lumins, I promise, we're much more refined!

Indeed, this great planet has creatures aplenty!
But for each of their skills, my dear, you have got twenty!

No, we're not the strongest, nor fastest! What's more,
Our teeth aren't the meanest! We don't even roar!

But we have this unique and invisible trait
That beats all the others and makes us so great!

So what is this thing that all Lumins possess,
That makes us so special, and drives our success?

Think hard now! Stay focused, and have a good ponder.
And while you are thinking, don't let your mind wander!

Perhaps you'll consider that magical space,
Where all of your thinking and pondering takes place!

That's it, now you've got it! You knew from the start!
What makes us so great is that we are so Smart!

We can sing!
We can dance!
We can surf on a wave!

We wash up and wear pants
and chew breath mints and shave!

We do science and math.
We send robots to Mars.

We design and build planes,
and we race in fast cars!

Just look at our cities!
Our bridges! Our trains!

Our greatest achieveme
are made with our bra

for **all** of your talents,
...hink that you'll find,

...at the best one of all
...our Brilliant mind!

Amazing you are,
from your head to your toe!

You're amazing each day,
and we thought you should know.